LEVEL 2

Administered by the Center for Civic Education
in cooperation with the National Conference of State Legislatures

We the People: Project Citizen

is directed by the Center for Civic Education
and funded by the U.S. Department of Education under the
Education for Democracy Act approved by the United States Congress.
For additional information please contact:

Project Citizen
Center for Civic Education
5145 Douglas Fir Road, Calabasas, CA 91302
818.591.9321 FAX 818.591.9330
www.civiced.org

Project Citizen
National Conference of State Legislatures
7700 East First Place, Denver, CO 80230
303.364.7700 FAX 303.364.7800
www.ncsl.org

12 11 10 01 02 03

ISBN 10 0-89818-215-8
ISBN 13 978-0-89818-215-6

A NOTE TO READERS

Dear Students, Teachers, and Parents:

We at the Center for Civic Education welcome your participation in **We the People: Project Citizen**, a program in public policy-making. We hope you will find it interesting and worthwhile.

In the words of Abraham Lincoln, we have inherited a government that is "of the people, by the people, for the people." Our right to participate in governing ourselves in order to protect our rights and promote our common welfare carries certain responsibilities. Among these responsibilities are the need to develop the knowledge and skills to participate intelligently and the willingness to promote liberty and justice for all people.

We believe this program will add to students' knowledge, enhance their skills, and deepen their understanding of how we can all work together to make our communities better.

We wish you well, and we hope that you find the program a stimulating and valuable experience.

Sincerely,

Charles N. Quigley
EXECUTIVE DIRECTOR

ACKNOWLEDGMENTS

Project Citizen Program Director
Michael G. Fischer

Curriculum Developers
Charles N. Quigley
Michael G. Fischer
Kenneth Rodriguez
Charles F. Bahmueller

Editorial Director
Mark Gage

Associate Editor
David Hargrove

Creative Director
Mark Stritzel

Illustrator
Richard Stein

Cover+Interior Design
Mark Stritzel

Production Designers
Sean Fay
Erin Breese

The Center is grateful for the helpful comments and suggestions received from the following persons who reviewed the manuscript in its various development stages. The Center has attempted to be responsive to the many valuable suggestions for improvement in the text. The final product, however, is the responsibility of the Center and does not necessarily reflect the views of those who have contributed their thoughts and ideas.

Contributing Writers and Reviewers

Ben Bohmfalk
Teacher, Basalt High School
Basalt, Colorado

Margaret Branson
Associate Director, Center for Civic Education
Reno, Nevada

Roger Desrosiers
Teacher
Millbury, Massachusetts

Kevin Fox
Teacher, Arcadia High School
Arcadia, California

Larry Gerston
Political Science Professor
San Jose State Univ., School of Social Science
San Jose, California

F. Klaus Koopmann
Professor, Department of Political Science
University of Bremen
Bremen, Germany

Barbara Miller
Executive Director
Center for Education in Law and Democracy
Denver, Colorado

Mark Miner
Teacher, Oconomowoc High School
Oconomowoc, Wisconsin

Diane Palmer
Project Citizen State Coordinator
Belmont, Massachusetts

Beth Ratway
Social Studies Consultant
Wisconsin Department of Public Instruction
Madison, Wisconsin

CONTENTS

CHAPTER 1
Introduction to Project Citizen

PURPOSE

This chapter provides brief descriptions of five concepts useful in describing and understanding the American political system. It also explains the goals of the Project Citizen program. When you have finished this chapter, you should be able to explain the five concepts and their implications. You should also be able to explain and evaluate the goals of Project Citizen.

A What Five Concepts Are Useful in Describing and Understanding the American Political System?

- **liberalism**
- **constitutionalism**
- **democracy**
- **republic**
- **federalism**

Put them together and the American political system can be described as a liberal, constitutional, democratic republic with a federal system of government.

Liberalism The term "liberal" is derived from the term "liberty." A liberal political system is one in which individual rights and freedoms are highly valued and protected. The Declaration of Independence states that "...all Men are endowed by their Creator with certain unalienable Rights, that among these are Life, Liberty, and the Pursuit of Happiness—That to secure these Rights, Governments are instituted among Men, deriving their just Powers from the Consent of the Governed...." These words focusing on individual rights and freedoms are evidence of the liberal nature of the American political system.

It is important to understand that the term "liberal" has several different meanings. As it is used in this text, it refers to liberty and it should not be confused with the use of the term "liberal" when it is used as opposed to "conservative" positions on social, economic, or political matters.

Constitutionalism Ours is a "constitutional government" because the U.S. Constitution serves as a higher law that everyone must obey including those serving in government. Constitutional government is limited government. Through the Constitution the people delegate powers to their government to enable it to serve the purposes for which it was established.

The major purposes of our government are clearly set forth in the second paragraph of the Declaration of Independence and the Preamble to the Constitution. The responsibility of government to fulfill these purposes is the reason the People agreed to its establishment and continued operation, and also why the People agree to abide by the laws established by their government.

> *We hold these Truths to be self-evident, that all Men are created equal, that they are endowed by their Creator with certain unalienable Rights, that among these are Life, Liberty, and the Pursuit of Happiness — That to secure these Rights, Governments are instituted among Men, deriving their just Powers from the Consent of the Governed ....*
>
> *Declaration of Independence*

> *We the people of the United States, in Order to form a more perfect Union, establish Justice, insure domestic Tranquility, provide for the common defence, promote the general Welfare, and secure the Blessings of Liberty to ourselves and our Posterity, do ordain and establish this Constitution for the United States of America.*
>
> *Preamble to the U.S. Constitution*

Together the Declaration and the Preamble make it clear that the major purposes of our government are

- To secure the unalienable rights of individuals such as those to life, liberty, property, and the pursuit of happiness
- To establish justice
- To provide for individual security and public order
- To protect the people from harm from internal and external sources
- To provide for the general welfare

Federalism We have a federal system of government (federalism) because power and responsibility are divided and shared between a national government having nationwide responsibilities and state and local governments having state and local responsibilities. This system provides

one means for limiting and checking the use of power because it is separated and shared among different levels of government. It is important to understand that the terms "democracy" and "republic" as used in this text refer to forms of government and not to the Democratic and Republican political parties in the United States.

Democracy We are a "democracy" because we believe in the idea of "popular sovereignty." Popular sovereignty means that the ultimate powers of government are held by the people who consent to delegate those powers to a government of their making, which they can alter or abolish, if it misuses or abuses the powers it has been delegated. We are also a democracy because all adult citizens, with few exceptions, can vote in free elections and hold public office.

Republic We are a "republic" (or a representative democracy) because in most cases decisions about government are made by representatives serving in governmental institutions rather than by direct vote of the people as would occur in a direct democracy.

B Class Activity — Demonstrating Understanding of Basic Concepts and Their Implications

Work with one or two other students to develop answers to the following questions. Then be prepared to present and discuss your answers with the entire class.

1 Give examples from the American political system of each of the five concepts that you have studied. What other terms or concepts might you use to describe the American political system?

2 What might be the advantages or disadvantages of each of the five concepts in protecting the rights of individuals?

3 In our democratic republic the people, through the U.S. Constitution and their state constitutions, have given the responsibility to make most decisions about government to their representatives. Why, then, should individuals participate in their government? Should they have the right not to participate? Explain.

4 If individuals wish to participate, what tools do they need to participate competently and responsibly?

C What Are the Purposes of Project Citizen?

Because the United States is a democratic republic, most decision-making and other work of government is accomplished by elected and appointed representatives. However, it has been recognized since the founding of our nation that the preservation and healthy functioning of our democracy requires that citizens play an active role in what is ultimately a system of self-government. For citizens to play such a role requires, among other things, that they

- understand their system of government;
- have the knowledge, skills, and willingness to participate to an adequate degree; and

- participate guided by an enlightened, reasoned commitment to the fundamental values and principles of American democracy.

The principal purpose of Project Citizen is to help you to improve your capacities to participate competently and responsibly in the American political system. In addition to the requirements noted above, such participation requires that you have the capacity to keep track of, or monitor, what your government is doing and to influence it on matters of concern to you.

In a country as large and complex as the United States, monitoring and influencing government is not always an easy task. Our federal system includes three branches of government (executive, legislative, and judicial branches) each at federal, state, and local levels and numerous affiliated agencies. In fact, there are more than 87,000 governments and governmental agencies in the United States. This system is challenging to citizens who are often confused about which level or levels of government and which branches or agencies of government are responsible for matters of interest to them.

Project Citizen provides a practical, first-hand approach to learning about our complex system of government and how to monitor and influence it. You will work together with other students in your class to conduct research in your community in order to discover problems that you think your governments are not handling at all or not handling well. Then you will select a problem from among those you have identified and work cooperatively to

- conduct research on the problem
- identify alternative solutions to the problem and weigh their advantages and disadvantages
- propose a solution to the problem that requires governmental action and does not violate provisions of your state and federal constitutions

- propose an action plan to influence the appropriate governmental agencies to consider or adopt your solution to the problem

Once these tasks are completed, you will record the results of your work on a portfolio and in a documentation binder. Then you will take part in a simulated public hearing in which you will present the results of your work to a panel of public and/or private sphere representatives of your community. If your class wishes to do so, you may also actively try to get government officials to consider or adopt the solutions to problems that you have proposed.

By taking part in Project Citizen, you will "learn by doing" the work of active citizens in your community. By completing your tasks, you should learn

- about the existence and roles of "civil society" (the sphere of voluntary activity in society) in the political process
- which branches, agencies, and levels of government have the authority and responsibility to deal with the problem you have chosen to work on
- how to monitor and influence the political process in your community, state, or nation

Although your attention may have been limited to one particular problem in your community or state, the knowledge and skills you gain are those required for competent and responsible participation throughout the American political system.

The sponsors of Project Citizen hope that the experiences and learning it fosters will encourage you to take an active role in the political life of your community, state, and nation. If the United States is to fulfill its historic mission of being a nation of, by, and for the people, dedicated to liberty and justice for all, it is essential that the people take part in their system of self-government.

D What Opinions and Knowledge Do You Have About Participation in the Political Life of Your Community?

Before taking the next steps in Project Citizen, write your answers to the questions on Form 1. These questions ask for opinions about the responsibilities of citizens in a democracy and knowledge about participation and its consequences. After you have filled out the form, ask several adults how they would answer the questions and record their answers.

Bring your findings to class to share and discuss the responses you have gathered. Keep a record of your responses so you can compare your answers to the same questions after you have finished Project Citizen.

FORM 1
PARTICIPATION IN DEMOCRACY

1 To what extent, if any, do citizens have a responsibility to take part in the civic life of their community?

- Ⓐ no responsibility
- Ⓑ some responsibility
- Ⓒ a large responsibility
- Ⓓ a very large responsibility

Explain your answer.

____

____

____

____

____

2 To what extent, if any, do citizens have a responsibility to participate in the public policymaking processes at local, state, and national levels?

- Ⓐ no responsibility
- Ⓑ some responsibility
- Ⓒ a large responsibility
- Ⓓ a very large responsibility

Explain your answer.

____

____

____

____

____

3 What can citizens do to monitor the development and implementation of public policy in their community?

____

____

____

____

____

4 What can citizens do to influence the development and implementation of public policy in their community?

____

____

____

____

____

5 How can citizens gain access to governmental agencies in their community, state, and nation?

6 In what ways can the voluntary organizations of civil society participate in the formulation and, in some instances, in the implementation of public policy?

7 What might be some consequences of an individual deciding not to participate in civic life? What might be the consequences if large numbers of individuals do not participate in civic life?

CHAPTER 2

An Introduction to Public Policy

PURPOSE

This chapter provides background information that is useful in understanding the meaning of the term "public policy" and the role of public policy in local, state, and national government. When you have completed this chapter you should be able identify the private sphere, civil society, and government as three parts of society. You should also be able to evaluate, take, and defend positions on which parts of society may be best suited to deal with certain problems. Finally, you should be able to explain the role of public policy in dealing with common problems of society.

A What Are the Private Sphere, Civil Society, and Government?

For the purposes of this project, it is useful to look at society as being composed of the following three areas or spheres.

Private sphere This is the part of society in which family and friends associate to pursue their private interests within the law, free of unreasonable and unfair intrusion by government

Civil society This is the part of society where people associate or interact voluntarily to pursue interests they share. They may do so as individuals or as members of social, economic, or political associations or organizations. Although these associations and organizations operate within legal limits, participation in them is not required by law and they are not part of government. Associations and organizations in civil society can provide an effective means for monitoring and influencing government. They may also provide a means of checking or limiting the use of power by government.

Government This part of society includes formal governmental institutions at local, state, and national levels. These include legislative, executive, and judicial branches of government at all three levels.

B Class Activity — Distinguishing Among Areas or Spheres of Society

Listed below are some everyday events that might occur in the United States. For each event, identify whether it takes place in Ⓐ the private sphere, Ⓑ civil society, Ⓒ government, or Ⓓ a combination of any of these.

1 A local school board changes graduation requirements.

Ⓐ Ⓑ Ⓒ Ⓓ

2 Susan becomes a member of the Girl Scouts.

Ⓐ Ⓑ Ⓒ Ⓓ

3 Carmen and her friend go out to dinner and a movie.

Ⓐ Ⓑ Ⓒ Ⓓ

4 Marco's family and friends have a picnic on July 4.

Ⓐ Ⓑ Ⓒ Ⓓ

5 Sara and her two sisters join a labor union.

6 The Sierra Club lobbies state legislators to pass environmental protection laws.

7 The state legislature passes a law limiting the use of cell phones while driving.

Ⓐ Ⓑ Ⓒ Ⓓ

8 Citizens join a taxpayer's association in an effort to get government to lower taxes.

9 The federal government awards a contract to a private company to repair sections of an interstate highway.

10 A city council passes a law establishing smoke free zones in public parks.

C Which Areas of Society Should Deal with Certain Problems?

Sometimes it is very clear what problems and issues should be dealt with by either the private sphere, civil society, governmental institutions or a combination of these areas or spheres of society. At other times, reasonable people may differ about which part of society should take responsibility for dealing with certain problems or types of problems. These differences might be based on personal opinions or philosophical positions about the proper role of government in society. Some people think government should take responsibility for a large range of problems in society while others think government should be limited to a smaller range and that many problems should be dealt with by civil society or individuals acting in the private sphere.

D Class Activity — Taking Positions on Which Area or Areas of Society Should Take Primary Responsibility for Dealing with Common Problems

The following are some common problems in society. For each problem, be prepared to take and defend a position on which of the following three parts of society or what combination of them should be primarily responsible for dealing with the problem: Ⓐ the private sphere, Ⓑ civil society, or Ⓒ government.

1. Ensuring that children from birth to three years old eat nutritious food and develop healthy hygiene habits

   Ⓐ Ⓑ Ⓒ

2. Ensuring that children receive equal educational opportunities

   Ⓐ Ⓑ Ⓒ

3. Promoting the moral development of young children

   Ⓐ Ⓑ Ⓒ

4. Caring for elderly poor people

   Ⓐ Ⓑ Ⓒ

5 Protecting the borders of the country

Ⓐ Ⓑ Ⓒ

6 Maintaining streets in cities and towns

Ⓐ Ⓑ Ⓒ

7 Providing medical care for the indigent

Ⓐ Ⓑ Ⓒ

8 Protecting people from criminal activity

Ⓐ Ⓑ Ⓒ

9 Upholding the moral standards of the community

Ⓐ Ⓑ Ⓒ

10 Building highways, bridges, and dams

Ⓐ Ⓑ Ⓒ

11 Protecting the country from external attack

Ⓐ Ⓑ Ⓒ

12 Promoting economic prosperity

Ⓐ Ⓑ Ⓒ

E What is Public Policy?

There are reasonable differences of opinion among scholars on the definition of the term "public policy." Because examining these differences would divert attention from the principal goals of Project Citizen, the definition stated below has been selected as most useful for the purposes of the project.

Definition and function of public policy

In democracies, a public policy is a concept or set of ideas that guides a course of action or a procedure used in dealing with public issues or problems.

Public policies are often embodied in laws, rules, or regulations or agreed upon procedures used by government to fulfill its responsibilities to protect the rights of the people and to promote the general welfare.

For example:

- all states have laws that provide for free public education for students of certain ages to provide them with the knowledge and skills required to be competent and responsible citizens and to be able to earn a living. These laws reflect a policy of respect for the rights of individuals to the "pursuit of happiness" and a concern with promoting the general welfare by encouraging the development of a society composed of knowledgeable, skilled, responsible, and self-reliant citizens.

Public policies serve to distribute certain benefits and burdens of society, manage the allocation of resources, and manage conflicts. For example, public policy

- provides all young people the benefit of a free public education and places upon taxpayers the burden of paying for it
- manages the use of public lands by lumber companies
- provides for a system of courts to manage conflicts among people

Governments at local, state, and national levels create public policies, carry them out, and manage disputes about them. For example:

- a local government might promote conservation by establishing a policy requiring people to separate recyclable trash from other trash
- a state government might hold hearings to listen to disputes among developers and environmentalists about the proper use of public lands

Implementation of public policies

Public policies may be implemented by

- governmental institutions acting alone, such as the federal government managing the distribution of Social Security benefits to eligible people
- governmental institutions acting cooperatively with civil society, such as agencies of the federal or state government awarding a contract to a private company to construct highways, bridges, dams, or airports

- governmental institutions and civil society acting independently, but dealing with the same problem. For example:
  - both local government and religious organizations might provide homeless shelters or child-care facilities
  - governmental agencies and charitable organizations such as the Red Cross might have independent programs designed to help people affected by natural disasters
- civil society handling problems not dealt with by government in accordance with a government policy. This leaves such problems to be dealt with by civil society or the private sphere. For example:
  - professional associations might provide special programs and training to enhance the knowledge and skills of their members
  - religious institutions might try to enhance the morality of their constituents

Procedural justice and the development and implementation of public policy

Procedural justice refers to the fairness of the ways information is gathered and the fairness of the ways decisions are made. In democracies, in particular, people working in governmental agencies and institutions, the "servants of the people," are required to use fair procedures in the development and implementation of public policy that, among other goals, enable the people to observe and take part in their government. The goals of procedural justice are to

- increase the chances of discovering information necessary to make wise and just decisions
- insure the wise and fair use of the information in making decisions
- protect important values and interests such as the right to privacy, human dignity, freedom, distributive justice, and efficiency

For procedures to be fair they should adhere to the following:

- **Be open to the public**
  Unless there is a very good reason for secrecy such as national defense or the protection of minor children, procedural justice should be open for all to witness. This is necessary to enable members of the public to be aware of what their government is doing and be able to influence it, if they wish to do so.
- **Provide relevant and accurate information to the public**
  Information should be provided if it is related to the development and implementation of public policy unless there is a very good reason for not doing so such as national security or the protection of basic rights of individuals.
- **Provide fair notice**
  People should be notified of the proposed actions of government that might affect them in adequate time for them to be prepared for what might take place.
- **Provide expert assistance when needed**
  People who wish to have a voice in a proposed action by government should have the right to the assistance of experts in relevant fields when they participate in the process, such as a translator or an attorney to help them present their position.
- **Provide the right to supportive witnesses and to examine opposing witnesses**
  People should have the right to the assistance of witnesses supporting their position and to examine witnesses opposing their position.
- **Provide the right to an impartial hearing**
  Decisions should be made by impartial third parties who do not stand to benefit from the outcome of their decisions.
- **Provide the right to appeal**
  People should have the right to appeal decisions by governmental agencies to an impartial agency.

F Class Activity — Applying the Definition of Public Policy

Which of the four descriptions below best categorizes the ten situations listed? Be prepared to explain your choice.

Ⓐ A public policy solution to a problem by a governmental institution

Ⓑ A public policy solution to a problem by a governmental institution cooperating with civil society

Ⓒ A solution to a problem dealt with by public policy and by civil society each acting independently

Ⓓ A solution to a problem by civil society acting alone

1 Government funding of medical research, interstate highways, and higher education

Ⓐ Ⓑ Ⓒ Ⓓ

2 Providing assistance to the poor through government issued food stamps and the voluntary contributions of church members

Ⓐ Ⓑ Ⓒ Ⓓ

3 Providing education by religious institutions to promote their specific moral standards

4 Creating the Department of Homeland Security by the federal government to protect the country from the threat of terrorism

Ⓐ Ⓑ Ⓒ Ⓓ

5 Community groups taking disadvantaged urban youth on rural outings

Ⓐ Ⓑ Ⓒ Ⓓ

6 Providing training to neighborhood watch groups by law enforcement agencies

Ⓐ Ⓑ Ⓒ Ⓓ

7 Providing food and shelter for the homeless by both state government and private groups

Ⓐ Ⓑ Ⓒ Ⓓ

8 Community groups arranging for young people to visit elderly members of the community who live alone and lack social contact

Ⓐ Ⓑ Ⓒ Ⓓ

9 Federal government providing tax incentives to businesses for them to locate in areas of high unemployment

Ⓐ Ⓑ Ⓒ Ⓓ

10 Authorizing public funding of charter schools by a board of education

Ⓐ Ⓑ Ⓒ Ⓓ

G Focusing on Public Policy Problems

In the United States and some other countries, the right to privacy and a private sphere of life free of interference by government is very important. These countries also have a highly developed civil society. In such countries, many problems are dealt with privately by individuals or civil society without involvement by government. In fact, it is public policy in the United States to leave some problems to civil society and/or the private sphere.

Some problems, however, are arguably more efficiently dealt with primarily by government with the cooperation of civil society or by government alone. Because the main purpose of this program is to help you learn about how your government works at local, state, and national levels and how to monitor and influence government at these levels, you will be asked to focus on public policy problems rather than problems dealt with by civil society or the private sphere acting alone.

H Class Activity — Creating Public Policy and Civil Society Solutions to Community Problems

Go to the middle column on the following chart and read the first example of a community problem. Look at the examples of a public policy solution to the problem by a governmental institution acting with or without civil society in column one, and a solution to the problem solely by civil society in column three. Then fill out the rest of the chart with your own suggestions for public policy and civil society solutions to the other problems. Use the last space to identify a problem in your own community and give examples of public policy and civil society solutions to it. After you fill in your chart, share your responses with your group members or classmates.

FORM 2

CREATING PUBLIC POLICY AND CIVIL SOCIETY SOLUTIONS TO COMMUNITY PROBLEMS

Read the first example of a community problem shown in the middle column below and the examples of (1) a public policy solution to the problem by a government institution acting with or without civic society and (2) a solution to the problem solely by civil society. Then fill out the rest of the chart with your own suggestions for public policy and civil society solutions to the problems noted. Use the last space to identify a problem in your community and give examples of public policy and civil society solutions for it. After you have come up with your responses, share them with your group members or classmates.

PUBLIC POLICY SOLUTION	COMMUNITY PROBLEMS	CIVIL SOCIETY SOLUTION
City officials fund a program to give needy individuals vouchers to use to "buy" food and clothing from participating merchants	Poor families in the community need food and adequate clothing	Members of a civic organization conduct a drive to collect food and clothing and then distribute it to the needy
	School-aged children are out on the streets late at night	
	Parents are not using child protective car seats properly	
	The lake in the community is polluted and filled with litter	
	Owners of a professional football team want to build a stadium in the city	
	Many local high school students have been cheating on homework and tests	

CHAPTER 3

The Project Citizen Process

PURPOSE

In this chapter you and your classmates will conduct an investigation into problems that face your community. You will be focusing on problems that require some degree of government action in order for there to be a successful resolution.

You will follow a six-step process that will enable you to identify and study one significant problem, recommend a solution in the form of a public policy proposal, and present your research and proposal in the form of a portfolio and public hearing.

STEPS

The six steps of the Project Citizen process, which are described in this chapter, are as follows:

Step 1 Identifying Problems to Be Dealt with by Public Policy

Step 2 Selecting a Problem or Problems for Your Class to Study

Step 3 Gathering Information on the Problem You Will Study

Step 4 Developing a Portfolio to Present Your Research

Step 5 Presenting Your Portfolio in a Simulated Public Hearing

Step 6 Reflecting on Your Experience

Category #
Levees
Category 5 #
Coastal Restoration
I
N.O.
CAT
AND
COASTA
5 LEVEES
AND
COASTAL
RESTORATION
gory 5 Levees
AND
al Restoration
NOW!!
ty Affiliation:
ouisianian
Cat 5 levees
AND

STEP 1

Identifying Problems to Be Dealt with by Public Policy

PURPOSE

In this step you will identify a number of problems in your community or state that you think should be dealt with primarily by government or by government and civil society acting cooperatively. These can be problems that you might have experienced or they might be problems that you have heard discussed by others; read about in the newspaper; or learned about from radio, television, or the Internet.

You also will learn something about each of the problems you have identified and which governmental agencies at local, state, or national levels might be responsible for dealing with those types of problems.

The purpose of this lesson is to prepare you for Step 2 when your class will select one problem to investigate further and propose a public policy solution to the problem as a part of your participation in Project Citizen.

A Small Group Activity — Identifying Problems in Your Community Requiring Public Policy Solutions

Every community, state, and nation faces problems that might require public policy solutions. The following are examples of some types of problems in the United States that often require public policy solutions.

- Providing safe, clean schools, and a good education for all students
- Supervising and caring for young people in the community
- Providing essential services to community members
- Promoting safety and security
- Promoting public health
- Promoting and maintaining jobs and businesses in the community
- Protecting the environment
- Maintaining community standards of decency
- Protecting basic rights of citizens

Work with one or two other students to identify three to five problems that exist in your school, neighborhood, city, county, or state. You may use the above list to help you identify such problems, or you may select other types of problems. Select one problem from your list that your group thinks might be a good one for you to study further. Remember that it must be a problem that can be addressed by a public policy. Record the results of your discussions and be prepared to present your findings to your class.

B Individual Activity — Conducting Survey Research in Your Community to Determine Public Opinion about the Problem You Have Selected

Each student should now use **Form 3: Interview Report Form** on pages 28–30 for gathering information on the problem his or her group has selected for further study.

The form should be used for interviewing other students, parents, neighbors, teachers, civic leaders, and other adult members of your community to find out

- if they think that the problem you have selected is important, and the reasons for their position
- if they believe the problem should be dealt with by government or by civil society or the private sphere or a combination of these areas, and why they think so
- if they think the problem should be dealt with by government, find out which level and agencies of government they think should be primarily responsible for dealing with the problem

Be prepared to present to your class the information you have found about the problem. Explain the problem and whether you think it should be dealt with by a public policy. If you think the problem should be dealt with by a public policy, try to identify which level of government and which agency has primary responsibility.

To find out what part of government might be responsible for dealing with the problem, you might

- ask assistance from the research desk at a public library
- search for the information on the websites of the executive branches of your local, state, and federal government—these will include the areas of public policy that each agency of government is responsible for handling
- use the sections on local, state, and the national government in your telephone book to identify which agencies might be responsible for dealing with the problems you have identified

Use **Form 4: Publications and/or Websites Report Form** on pages 31–33 to record information gained from those sources.

FORM 3
INTERVIEW REPORT FORM

Your name ______________________________

Before beginning the interview be sure to identify yourself and briefly explain the problem you are researching, why you chose to research this problem, and why you are conducting this interview. Before beginning, ask the person's permission to use her or his name. If a person does not wish to be named, respect her or his privacy and indicate only the person's role in the community.

1 Name and title of person being interviewed

____

____

2 The person's role in the community (e.g., parent, community volunteer, business person, retired person)

____

____

3 Explain the problem you are studying to the person you are interviewing.

____

____

____

____

4 Use the following questions in conducting the interview. Write or record the answers you receive.

a Do you think the problem I have described is important? Why?

____

____

____

____

b Do you think others in our community believe this is an important problem? Why?

____

____

____

____

c What might be the cause or causes of the problem?

____

____

____

____

d Do you think this is a problem that should be dealt with by

- government acting alone? Why or why not?

- government with the assistance of civil society? Why or why not?

- government with the assistance of the private sphere? Why or why not?

- government with the assistance of civil society and the private sphere? Why or why not?

e What policy, if any, is already in place to deal with this problem?

f If a policy does exist, ask the following questions.

- What are the advantages of this policy?

- What are the disadvantages of this policy?

- How might the policy be improved?

FORM 3

INTERVIEW REPORT FORM (CONTINUED)

- Does it need to be replaced? Why?

- What disagreements about this policy, if any, exist in our community?

g If there is no policy currently in place to deal with the problem, ask the following questions.

- What sort of policy do you think might be needed to address the problem?

- What level(s), branch(es), or agency(ies) of government are responsible, or should be responsible, for dealing with the problem?

5 Do you have any suggestions for where I might get more information about this problem and the different positions people take on the problem?

FORM 4

PUBLICATIONS AND/OR WEBSITES REPORT FORM

Problems Facing Your Community

Use a separate form for each publication or website.

Your name ______________________________

1 Briefly describe the problem you are researching.

____

____

____

____

2 List the title, author, date of publication, publisher or URL address of the website that you used in your research.

____

____

3 Explain what information, if any, the publication or website offers to explain why the problem you have selected is important.

____

____

____

4 Explain whether the information you have read leads you to believe that this is a problem that should be dealt with by

a government acting alone? Why or why not?

____

____

____

b government with the assistance of civil society? Why or why not?

____

____

____

c government with the assistance of the private sphere? Why or why not?

____

____

____

d government with the assistance of civil society and the private sphere? Why or why not?

____

____

____

FORM 4
PUBLICATIONS AND/OR WEBSITES REPORT FORM (CONTINUED)

Answer the following questions about the information you found.

1 What position does the publication or website take regarding the problem?

____

2 Summarize the essential points of the position.

____

3 According to the publication or website, what policy, if any, does government now have to deal with the problem?

____

4 If a policy does exist, provide any information it includes on the following questions.

a What are the advantages of the policy?

____

b What are the disadvantages of the policy?

____

c How might the policy be improved?

____

d Does it need to be replaced? Why?

____

e What disagreements about the policy, if any, exist in our community?

____
____
____
____

5 If a policy does not exist and the publication or website presents a proposed policy, record any information provided on the following questions.

a What are the advantages of the proposed policy?

____
____
____
____

b What are the disadvantages of the proposed policy?

____
____
____
____

c What disagreements might there be to the proposed policy?

____
____
____
____

6 Summarize the most important information you were able to obtain from this publication or website.

____
____
____
____
____
____
____
____

7 Does the publication or website suggest other sources of information? If so, what are they?

____
____
____
____

C Small Group Activity — Learning More about the Problems the Class Has Identified

Your teacher should divide the class into small study groups of four to six students each. Each group should

1. discuss the problems that the individual members have studied
2. choose one problem that the group recommends the entire class work on to complete the tasks of Project Citizen, and
3. select one student to present the group's choice to the rest of the class and explain the reason for their choice.

This information will be used in Step 4.

★ **Note**

Keep all of the information you have gathered in this step and the remaining steps to use in completing the tasks of Project Citizen.

STEP 2

Selecting a Problem or Problems for Your Class to Study

PURPOSE

In this step your entire class will discuss the problems the study groups have researched. When there is enough information to select a single problem for further study, the class as a whole will be asked to conduct in-depth research into the problem selected.

A Sharing Information on Community Problems and Recommending a Problem to Study

In the last step, your study group investigated one problem facing your community.

A representative of each study group should now be asked to make a report to the rest of the class, sharing what the group has learned about the problem it studied.

Then, each study group should make a recommendation for or against the class taking on the problem it has selected for in-depth research.

- All problems recommended should require the use of public policy in their solution.
- These policies might involve action solely by government or by government working cooperatively with civil society and/or the private sphere.

B Selecting a Problem for the Class to Study

The class should then select one problem for the entire class to study. After the choice has been made, the problem should be reviewed so everyone clearly understands what he or she will be working on.

Use the following criteria to guide you in the selection of a problem for the class to study.

Be sure that it is a problem that

- Should be addressed or resolved by government acting alone, or by government acting in cooperation with civil society or the private sphere
- Is important to you and your community
- You can gather enough information about to develop a good project
- You might actually be able to address or resolve by proposing a public policy to government officials in your community, state, or federal government

STEP 3

Gathering Information on the Problem You Will Study

PURPOSE

Now that your class has selected a problem, you must decide where to get additional information. You already have some information on the problem that you gathered in the initial stages of investigating problems in your community (Step 1).

In this step, you will conduct additional research on the problem your class is studying. You will use a variety of resources including media sources, printed material, the Internet, and individuals with special knowledge related to the problem.

A Why It Is Important to Gather Information from a Variety of Sources

To develop a good understanding of a problem, it is important to gather information from a number of sources. Then you need to compare this information and use what seems most reliable to develop an accurate description of the problem. In comparing information from different sources, you will find that some sources are more reliable than others but that many, or all, might have something to contribute to an understanding of the problem.

You will also find that different sources may take different positions on problems that reflect different interests, goals, and priorities. For example, if you have selected an environmental problem you will discover that environmentalists are likely to have very different views and positions on the problem than developers or other business interests.

B Class Activity — Identifying Sources of Information

On the next two pages there is a list of some sources of information you should explore. Read and discuss the list. Identify specific sources or individuals that you want to use or contact. You will find that some sources of information are better than others, depending on the problem you are studying. For example, if you have selected a problem related to providing public services, you will find certain individuals and groups know more about problems of public services in your community than others. You might also find that some of the sources identified below may not be relevant to the problem you are studying.

You might also invite individuals to visit your class to share what they know about the problem you are researching. People who have special knowledge or expertise related to your problem, or representatives of interest groups in civil society that deal with your type of problem would be best. Save all the information you gather for use in the development of the portfolio described in Step 3.

Examples of sources of information

Libraries Libraries in your community may have newspapers, magazines, journals, books, and other publications with information about the problem you are researching.

Internet You should be able to find many useful websites from government agencies and private sphere organizations with information related to the problem you have selected.

Newspapers Newspapers commonly provide information on problems in their communities and what government is doing about them. You may also access newspapers via the Internet. Many newspapers maintain online archives of articles and stories they have run.

Professors and Scholars Professors in local colleges or universities may be experts on the problem you are studying. Most colleges and universities have a website that contains links to its academic schools, departments, and faculty members. A phone book will also list the public information offices of nearby colleges and universities. You can call those offices for help in locating scholars who might be helpful.

Lawyers and Judges Depending on the problem you are researching, lawyers and judges may be excellent sources of information. Also, most lawyers and judges belong to state and local bar associations that may provide some free services to the public. Many bar associations maintain websites that identify their members and list their special areas of legal expertise. These sites may be accessible to the public. You can use a phone book to identify local and state bar associations.

Interest Groups and Other Community Organizations
Many interest groups and community organizations have been formed to take action related to problems found in our communities. Some groups might have offices in your community. Use the Internet or a phone directory to find information about local offices/chapters and individuals associated with interest groups or other community groups that deal with the problem you have selected.

Legislative Offices Your representatives in local and state legislatures and the United States Congress are responsible for identifying problems at local, state, and national levels and suggesting or supporting public policies to deal with them. Your representatives may have a district office in your community. You can find the address and phone numbers of these offices on the Internet or in a telephone book. These offices will have one or more people on staff who are responsible for helping constituents obtain information about problems and public policies in your community, state, or the nation. They may be able to help you obtain briefing papers, policy statements, or specific legislation on the problem you are researching.

Administrative Offices People working in administrative agencies of your local, state, and national government may be responsible for dealing with the problem your class has chosen to study. Public information offices of these agencies can provide information on the problem and what the government is doing about it. For example, your local government may have a health department or a building safety department. Use an Internet directory or a telephone book to find these or other appropriate government offices.

Guidelines for Obtaining and Documenting Information

The members of your class should divide into research groups after deciding what sources of information you will pursue. Each research group should be responsible for gathering information from two or more sources. For example, one research group could be responsible for contacting libraries and administrative agencies.

★ Note

Forms to use in gathering and recording information from different sources are included on pages 42–51.

If you are the person in your research group assigned to contact one of the sources of information described above, begin by introducing yourself. Inform the person of your purpose or why you are contacting him or her. Use the guidelines on Form 5, page 42, for introducing yourself.

People working in the places where you can find information are usually very busy. It is important to follow the suggestions given in the next column to avoid having your class place too much of a burden on the offices and individuals being asked for information.

1. **Calling sources on the phone**
   No more than one student should be given the assignment of calling any office for information. It is important, therefore, that the student who calls clearly records the information gained during a phone interview.

2. **Making appointments and interviewing people**
   One student should call to arrange for an appointment. A small group may visit an office or person to conduct a personal interview.

3. **Writing and requesting information**
   One or more students may write a letter requesting information from each office or person. Including a self-addressed stamped envelope may help you get a response.

FORM 5
GUIDELINES FOR INTRODUCING YOURSELF FOR INTERVIEWS

My name is (your name) ______________________________

I am a (grade level) student at (name of school) ______________________________

I am taking a (name of class) ______________________________

We are studying local problems, how they are dealt with by government, and how citizens can participate in their government.

The problem I am studying is… (briefly describe the problem)

____
____
____
____
____
____

I am responsible for finding out information about the problem to share with my class.

May I ask you a few questions now, or is there another time that would be better for me to call?

____
____
____

Is there another person I should call?

____
____
____

Do you have any printed information on the problem that you can send me? (If you are calling on the phone and the answer is yes, be prepared to give the person the address of your school.)

Is this information available electronically by email or on a website?

____
____
____

How may I access the information?

____
____
____
____

FORM 6

DOCUMENTATION OF INFORMATION FROM PRINTED PUBLICATIONS

1 Names of research group members

____

____

2 Date ______________________________

3 Briefly describe the problem you are researching.

____

____

____

____

____

____

4 Identify the library, office, agency, organization, or website where you obtained the publication.

____

5 Identify the

- title of the publication ______________________________
- author(s) ______________________________
- date of publication ______________________________

6 Use the information in the publication to answer as many of the following questions as you can.

a What community(ies) is/are affected by this problem?

____

____

____

____

b How serious is the problem in the community?

____

____

____

____

c How widespread is the problem in other communities and states?

____

____

____

____

FORM 6

DOCUMENTATION OF INFORMATION FROM PRINTED PUBLICATIONS (CONTINUED)

d Is there a public policy that deals with the problem? Yes ❐ No ❐

If yes, answer the following questions.

- What form does it take? (law, administrative regulation or order, judicial decision, other)

  ____

  ____

- Briefly describe the public policy. Does it involve action by government, civil society, the private sphere, or two or more of these?

  ____

  ____

  ____

- Is the public policy for dealing with the problem inadequate? Explain why.

  ____

  ____

  ____

- If the public policy for dealing with the problem is adequate, is it being poorly implemented or not enforced? Explain why.

  ____

  ____

  ____

If there is no policy dealing with the problem, explain why you think there is no policy.

____

____

____

____

e What level(s) and branch(es) of government is/are responsible for dealing with the problem?

____

____

____

____

f What, if anything, is currently being doing done by government to address this problem?

____

____

____

FORM 6

DOCUMENTATION OF INFORMATION FROM PRINTED PUBLICATIONS (CONTINUED)

g What disagreements about this public policy, or the current way of dealing with it, exist in the community?

____
____
____

h Who are the major individuals, groups, or organizations expressing opinions regarding the problem?

____
____
____

- What is their interest in the problem?

  ____
  ____
  ____

- What positions are they taking?

  ____
  ____
  ____

- What are the benefits and costs associated with their positions?

  ____
  ____
  ____

- How are they trying to influence government to adopt their position on the problem?

  ____
  ____
  ____

7 If your class develops a policy to deal with this problem, how might you influence government to adopt your policy?

____
____
____
____
____
____
____
____

FORM 7
DOCUMENTATION OF INFORMATION FROM INTERVIEWS OR LETTERS

1 Names of research group members

____

____

____

2 Date ______________________________

3 Briefly describe the problem you are researching.

____

____

____

____

____

4 Source of information

- Name ______________________________
- Title and organization ______________________________
- Address ______________________________
- Phone ______________________________

5 After introducing yourself and your task, briefly describe the problem you are studying and then ask the following questions.

a How serious do you believe this problem is in our community?

____

____

____

____

b How widespread is the problem in the community?

____

____

____

c What might be the cause or causes of the problem?

____

____

____

d Is there a public policy that deals with the problem? Yes ❒ No ❒

____

____

____

FORM 7

DOCUMENTATION OF INFORMATION FROM INTERVIEWS OR LETTERS (CONTINUED)

6 If there a public policy that deals with the problem, answer the following questions.

a What form does it take (law, regulation, governmental order, other)?

____

____

____

b Can you describe the public policy?

____

____

____

c Is the public policy for dealing with the problem inadequate?
Briefly, explain why.

____

____

____

d If the public policy for dealing with the problem is adequate,
is it being poorly implemented or not enforced? Briefly explain.

____

____

____

e If no, why do you think there is no policy at this time?

____

____

____

7 Do you think that this is a problem that should be handled by government? Why?

____

____

____

8 What level and branch of government or governmental agency,
if any, is responsible for dealing with the problem?

____

____

9 What is the government currently doing about the problem?

____

____

____

FORM 7

DOCUMENTATION OF INFORMATION FROM INTERVIEWS OR LETTERS (CONTINUED)

10 Should the government seek the assistance of civil society and/or the private sphere in dealing with the problem? Why or why not?

____

____

____

11 What disagreements, if any, exist in the community about this problem?

____

____

____

12 Who are the major individuals, groups, or organizations taking sides on the problem?

____

____

____

a What is their interest in the problem?

____

____

____

b What positions are they taking?

____

____

____

c What are the advantages and disadvantages of their positions?

____

____

____

d How are they trying to influence government to adopt their solutions to the problem?

____

____

____

13 If my class, or group, develops a policy to deal with this problem, how might we influence government to adopt our policy?

____

____

____

FORM 8
DOCUMENTATION OF INFORMATION FROM THE INTERNET

1 Names of research group members

____

____

____

2 Briefly describe the problem you are researching.

____

____

____

____

3 Identify the website where you found the information.

- Name of website and organization sponsoring it ______________________________
- URL address of the site ______________________________
- Author (if noted) of the information that is posted ______________________________
- Date the information was posted ______________________________

4 Use the information on the website to answer the following questions.

a What communities are being affected by this problem (school, neighborhood, city, county, state, nation)?

____

____

b How serious is the problem in the community?

____

____

____

____

c What might be the cause or causes of the problem?

____

____

____

____

d Is there a public policy that deals with the problem? Yes ❒ No ❒
If yes, answer the following questions:

- What form does it take (law, regulation, governmental order, other)?

____

____

____

- Briefly describe the public policy.

- Is the public policy for dealing with the problem inadequate? Briefly, explain why.

- If the public policy for dealing with the problem is adequate, is it not being well implemented or enforced? Briefly explain.

e If no, why do you think there is no policy at this time?

f What level and branch of government or governmental agency is responsible for dealing with the problem?

g What, if anything, is currently being done by government to address this problem?

FORM 8
DOCUMENTATION OF INFORMATION FROM THE INTERNET (CONTINUED)

h What disagreements about this public policy or the current way of dealing with it exist in the community?

i Who are the major individuals, groups, or organizations expressing opinions regarding the problem?

- What is their interest in the problem?

- What positions are they taking?

- What are the advantages and disadvantages associated with their positions?

- How are they trying to influence government to adopt their position on the problem?

C Analyzing the Information You Have Gathered

The entire class should work together to use the information they placed on Documentation Form 6 (Information from Printed Publications), Documentation Form 7 (Information from Interviews or Letters), and Documentation Form 8 (Information from the Internet) in filling out the following Form 9. In doing so, the class should be selective and only include information related to the problem, taking into account such factors as the reliability and comprehensiveness of the information you have gathered.

D Developing a Portfolio and Presentation

To prepare for Step 4, the entire class should work together to record their responses. In Step 4, the class will be organized into four working groups, each assigned to work on one of the following four tasks.

1. **Explain the problem**

   Record the description of the problem, its importance, and the need for a solution developed in Form 9.

2. **Identify alternative policy solutions to the problem and their advantages and disadvantages**

   Record the proposed policy solutions from Form 9 and discuss what advantages and disadvantages each might present.

3. **Develop a public policy solution for the class to propose**

   First review the meaning of the term public policy you studied in Chapter 2. Then draft a proposed public policy solution to the problem. Explain the advantages and disadvantages of the proposed policy. Suggest what level or levels of government and what agencies of government should be responsible for implementing the policy.

4. **Develop an action plan that lists the steps your class should take to gain government acceptance of the policy you are proposing**

   For some ideas on what might be done, refer to Form 9 where you recorded steps others have taken to get government to implement their policies.

FORM 9
ANALYZING INFORMATION ABOUT THE PROBLEM

1 Date ______________________________

2 List the sources of information used to fill out Forms 6, 7, and 8.

____

____

3 Use the information on Forms 6, 7, and 8 to complete the following tasks.

a State the problem clearly and concisely.

____

____

b Explain the importance of the problem and the need to deal with it. Answer the following questions in doing so.

- How serious is the problem?

  ____

  ____

- How widespread is the problem?

  ____

  ____

- How urgent is the need to address the problem?

  ____

  ____

c Is there a public policy that deals with the problem? Yes ❐ No ❐

If there is a policy, answer the following questions.

- Is the policy in a law, regulation, governmental order, or other?

  ____

  ____

- What is the public policy?

  ____

  ____

- Is the public policy inadequate? Explain why.

  ____

  ____

- Is the policy adequate but not being enforced? Briefly, explain.

  ____

  ____

If there is not a policy, why do you think this is true?

d What level and branch of government, or governmental agency, should be responsible for dealing with the problem?

e What, if anything, is the government currently doing about the problem?

f Should the government seek the assistance of civil society and/or the private sphere in dealing with the problem? Why?

g Who are the major individuals, groups, or organizations taking sides on the problem?

- What is their interest in the problem?
- What solutions are they suggesting?
- What are the advantages and disadvantages of their solutions?
- How are they trying to influence government to adopt their solutions to the problem?

h If your class develops a policy to deal with this problem, how might you influence government to adopt your policy?

STEP 4

Developing a Portfolio to Present Your Research

PURPOSE

Now that your class has completed Step 3, you are ready to begin to develop a portfolio. The portfolio should contain two basic elements: a visual display section and a document folder. These elements will each contain four parts corresponding to the four tasks completed at the end of Step 3. Your class will be divided into four groups. Each group will be responsible for creating one of the four parts of the portfolio.

A Portfolio Development Tasks

The following are the tasks of each of the four groups.

PORTFOLIO GROUP 1
Explaining the problem

This group is responsible for developing a detailed explanation of the problem the class has chosen to study. This explanation should state why the problem is important and which levels and branches of government, or governmental agencies, should deal with it.

PORTFOLIO GROUP 2
Evaluating alternative policies to deal with the problem

This group is responsible for explaining current and/or proposed alternative policies designed to solve the problem.

PORTFOLIO GROUP 3
Developing a public policy the class supports

This group is responsible for developing and justifying a specific public policy that the class is proposing and agrees to support. The group must also make the case that its proposed public policy serves the purposes of government set forth in the U.S. Constitution and does not violate the limits it places upon the powers of government. Students may also refer to their state constitutions that typically state similar purposes.

PORTFOLIO GROUP 4
Developing an action plan to gain government acceptance of the class policy

This group is responsible for developing an action plan showing how the class can influence their government to adopt the policy that it is proposing.

In addition to completing its own tasks, each of the four groups should communicate with the others so that when the class portfolio is completed and presentations are made, they will be well organized, coherent, and consistent.

B Specifications for Portfolios

FOUR-PANEL DISPLAY

The work of each of the four groups should be placed on a separate panel of a four-panel display. The display should be composed of four sheets of poster board, foam-core board, or the equivalent (approximately 32" wide by 40" high). The display should be developed so it can be placed on a table, bulletin board, or easel. Materials to be displayed may include such items as written statements, list of sources, charts, graphs, photographs, original art work, etc. (See illustration on page 72.)

DOCUMENTATION SECTION

Each of the four task groups should select additional materials from those gathered that best document their work and place them in a three-ring binder. Use dividers to separate the four sections containing each group's work. Include a table of contents for the binder and each section in it.

C Portfolio Evaluation Criteria

The following is a Portfolio Criteria Checklist that will help you develop a good portfolio. Use it as a guide while you are developing your portfolio. In addition to the items described in the Portfolio Criteria Checklist, you should consider the overall effect of your portfolio. Your portfolio should be well designed and show creativity and originality.

If your class enters its portfolio in a showcase or competition with other classes, a panel of judges will consider the Portfolio Criteria Checklist as they evaluate your portfolio. They will give separate ratings to each of the sections and to the portfolio as a whole.

Alternatives for Presenting Your Research

Developing a four-panel portfolio display with a documentation binder is one method of presenting the four parts of your Project Citizen portfolio. There are several other ways to present the work that you might want to consider.

- **Develop a computer-based presentation**
  Use a computer software program to prepare and present your portfolio. Examples of such programs are HyperStudio and PowerPoint.

- **Create a website**

- **Develop a web-based portfolio**
  Your homepage should provide links to the written and visual material in the four parts of the portfolio. Also, use links to specific sources of information and other relevant websites that you used in your research. Be sure to obtain written permission for the use of any copyrighted material you intend to display.

- **Produce a videotape ★**
  Create a videotape to present your portfolio. Prepare a script with a narrative, dialogue, and related visuals. Be sure to obtain any required written permission before taping at a site. You should request permission to tape individuals. You will need to have a written release signed by a parent or guardian to include any person under the age of 18 in your videotape.

★ Your videotape should be at least 30 minutes, but no longer than 60 minutes, in length. It should include title frames, credits, appropriate source citations, and notices of permission to use copyrighted material.

Portfolio Criteria Checklist

Use the following criteria to evaluate each section of your portfolio as you develop it.

SECTION ONE
Understanding the Problem

Does your portfolio

- state and explain the problem and its causes and present evidence that there is a problem?
- demonstrate an understanding of the issue(s) involved in the problem?
- demonstrate an understanding of existing or proposed public policies?
- explain disagreements about the problem that may exist in the community?
- explain why government should be involved in the solution?
- present information in the display and binder that correlates to and supports one another?

SECTION TWO
Analyzing Alternative Policies

Does your portfolio

- present two or three alternative policies to address the problem?
- explain advantages and disadvantages of each alternative policy presented?
- identify controversies and conflicts that need to be addressed for each alternative policy?
- present information in the display and binder that correlates to and supports one another?

SECTION THREE
Public Policy Development and Persuasiveness

Does your portfolio

- state a public policy that addresses the problem and identify the government branch or agency responsible for enacting the proposed public policy?
- support the proposed public policy with reasoning and evidence?
- identify advantages and disadvantages of the proposed public policy?
- explain and support your reasons why the proposed public policy serves the purposes of government set forth in the U.S. Constitution and does not violate the limits it places on government?
- present information in the display and binder that correlates to and supports one another?

SECTION FOUR
Implementation of the Action Plan

Has your group

- identified individuals and groups, both supporters and opponents, who will need to be influenced?
- identified government officials, both supporters and opponents, who will need to be influenced?
- outlined and explained an action process for getting the proposed public policy enacted?
- proposed actions that build and expand on work presented in previous panels or groups?
- presented information in the display and binder that correlates to and supports one another?

OVERALL PORTFOLIO

Does your completed portfolio

- construct a convincing and clear sequence from one panel/group to the next?
- use and document research from multiple sources and provide appropriate notation for the sources and research evidence used?
- use standards of good writing and good oral presentation, such as pacing, projection, articulation, poise, and eye contact?
- use relevant and appropriate graphics and written information?
- have visual appeal?
- include evidence of student reflection that states what students have learned?

D Instructions for Groups

The instructions for each group below specify in more detail what the groups are expected to accomplish in their sections of the portfolio. Although each group has its own responsibilities, groups should communicate with one another to share ideas and information. Group work should begin by reviewing and using the material the entire class developed in filling out Form 9 in Step 6. The work of each group should not be limited to what is included in Form 9. It should be considered as a resource for each group to use in initiating its work. Each group may need to do additional research to complete its tasks.

As each group works, there is a need to continue to work cooperatively with the other groups as they proceed so the class portfolio is coherent and comprehensive. Each group should have regular opportunities to inform the rest of the class of the progress being made.

It is also important that the groups collaborate as they decide what specific items should be included in the display and documentation sections of the portfolio. This collaboration will avoid displaying the same information more than once and guarantee the inclusion of the best materials.

PORTFOLIO GROUP 1

EXPLAINING THE PROBLEM

This group is responsible for explaining the problem in the first display and documentation sections of the portfolio.

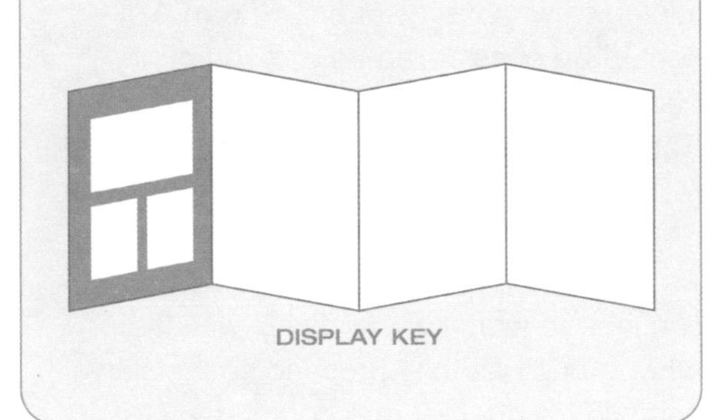

A DISPLAY SECTION 1

This part should include the following items:

1 **A written summary of the problem**
Review material gathered by research groups. Write no more than two double-spaced typed pages/script explaining the problem. Summarize what you have learned in response to the following questions.

- How serious is this problem in your community?
- How widespread is the problem in your school, neighborhood, city, state, or nation?
- Why is this a problem that should be handled by government? Should anyone else in the community also take responsibility for solving the problem? Why?
- Which of the following do you think is true? Explain your response.

- There is no public policy for dealing with the problem.
- The public policy for dealing with the problem is not adequate.
- The public policy for dealing with the problem is adequate, but it is not being well implemented or enforced.

- What disagreements, if any, exist in your community about the problem and the way it is being handled?
- Who are the major individuals, groups, or organizations with an interest in the problem?
- What is their interest?
- What positions are they taking?
- What are the advantages and disadvantages of their positions?
- How are they trying to influence government to adopt their views?
- What level and branch of government or governmental agency, if any, is responsible for dealing with the problem? What is it doing about the problem?

2 **Graphic presentations of the problem** These may include charts, graphs, photos, political cartoons, newspaper headlines, tables of statistics, and other illustrations. Illustrations may be from printed sources or they may be your original creations. Each illustration should have a caption or title and a source citation where appropriate.

3 **Identification of your sources of information** Include a bibliography identifying all sources used.

B DOCUMENTATION SECTION 1

Regardless of the presentation format your class chooses to present its work, you will need to create a documentation section in the form of a three-ring binder that includes copies of the best or most important information your class, or small group, gathered and used in your examination and explanation of the problem.

For example, you may include selected

- newspaper or magazine clippings
- written reports of interviews with people in the community
- written reports of radio and television coverage of the problem
- communications from public and private interest groups
- excerpts from government publications

Lengthy documents and reports should be represented by copies of their title pages, tables of contents, and a one-page summary (or abstract) of the document either taken from the document itself or written by the group. Be sure to prepare a table of contents for this section.

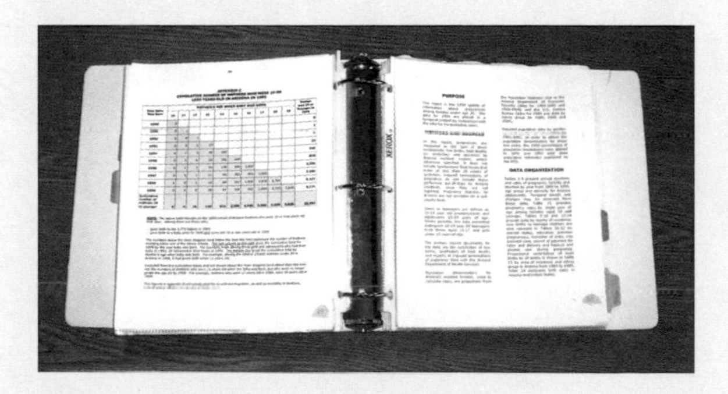

PORTFOLIO GROUP 2

EXAMINING ALTERNATIVE POLICIES TO DEAL WITH THE PROBLEM

This group is responsible for clearly explaining and evaluating present and/or alternative policies designed to deal with the problem. This group's findings are presented in the second display and documentation sections of the portfolio.

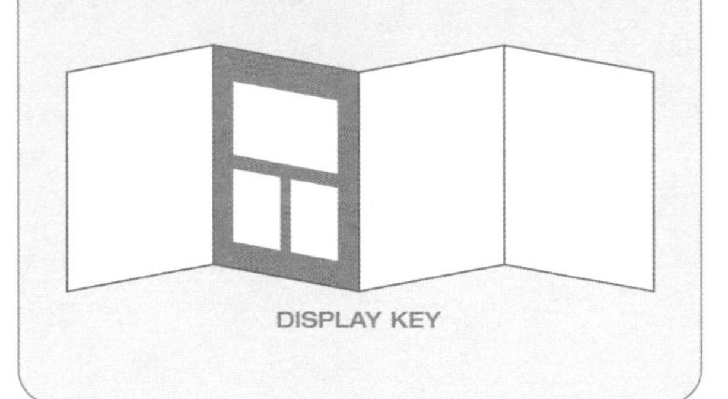

DISPLAY KEY

A DISPLAY SECTION 2

This part should include the following items.

1 **A written summary of alternative policies**
Identify two or three alternative public policies for dealing with the problem. These may include an existing policy or others being proposed by individuals or groups in the community. For each public policy presented, include no more than one double-spaced typed page/script that summarizes your answers to the following questions:

- What is the existing public policy, or the policy being proposed by an individual or group?
- What are the advantages and disadvantages of this policy?

2 **Graphic presentations of the policies**
These may include charts, graphs, photos, drawings, political cartoons, newspaper headlines, tables of statistics, and other illustrations related to the policies. These illustrations may come from printed sources or they may be your original creations. Each illustration should have a caption or title and a source citation where appropriate.

3 **Identification of your sources of information**
Include a bibliography identifying all sources used.

B DOCUMENTATION SECTION 2

Regardless of the presentation format your class or small group chooses to present its work, you will need to create a documentation section in the form of a three-ring binder that includes the best or most important information your class, or group, gathered and used in examining and evaluating present and alternative policies to deal with the problem.

For example, you may include as documentation

- selected newspaper or magazine clippings
- written reports or summaries of interviews with people in the community
- written reports of radio and television coverage of the problem
- communications from public and private interest groups
- excerpts from government publications

Lengthy documents and reports should be represented by copies of their title pages, tables of contents, and a one-page summary (or abstract) of the document either taken from the document itself or written by the group. Be sure to prepare a table of contents for this section.

PORTFOLIO GROUP 3

PROPOSING A PUBLIC POLICY TO DEAL WITH THE PROBLEM

This group is responsible for proposing a public policy to deal with the problem. The public policy your group chooses must be agreed to by a majority of the class or small group. It must also be a policy that does not violate your federal or state constitution. A Constitutional Opinion Form is included on pages 67–68 to assist in making sure your policy does not violate the U.S. Constitution or your state constitution. Once this is decided, your class, or small group, may choose to

- support one of the alternative policies identified by Portfolio Group 2
- modify one of those policies
- combine aspects of several of the alternatives
- develop your own public policy

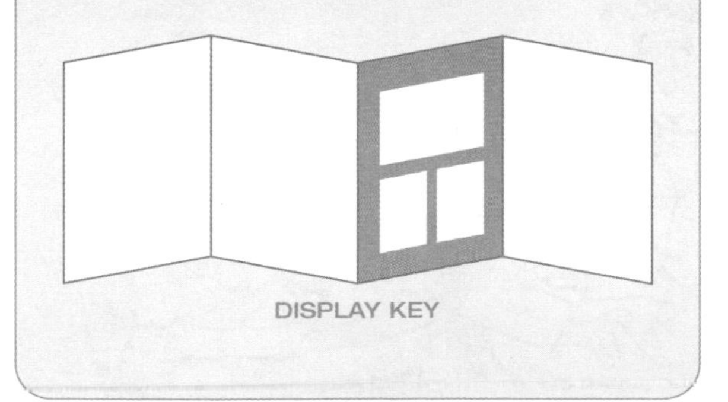

DISPLAY KEY

A DISPLAY SECTION 3

This part should include the following items:

1 **A written explanation and justification for your proposed public policy**
You should explain the public policy your class, or group, has developed and your reasons for supporting it. In no more than two double-spaced typed pages

- describe the public policy your class, or group, believes will best deal with the problem
- explain the advantages and disadvantages of your proposed public policy
- use the Constitutional Opinion Form on pages 67–68 to record your explanation of how and why your proposed public policy serves the purposes of government set forth in the Preamble to the U.S. Constitution and does not ask government to do something prohibited by the U.S. Constitution
- list the branch or agency and level of government that should be responsible for carrying out your proposed public policy
- explain whether your public policy should involve the assistance of civil society and/or the private sphere and your reasons

2 **Graphic presentations of your proposed public policy**
These may include charts, graphs, photos, drawings, political cartoons, newspaper headlines, tables of statistics, and other illustrations related to the policy and the problem it is designed to solve. These illustrations may come from printed sources or they may be your original creations. Each illustration should have a caption or title and a source citation where appropriate.

3 **Identification of your sources of information**
Include a bibliography identifying all sources used.

B DOCUMENTATION SECTION 3

Regardless of the presentation format your class or small group chooses to present its work, you will need to create a documentation section in the form of a three-ring binder that includes the best or most important information your class, or group, gathered and used in developing its proposed public policy.

For example, you may include as documentation

- selected newspaper or magazine clippings
- written reports or summaries of interviews with people in the community
- written reports of radio and television coverage of the problem
- communications from public and private interest groups
- excerpts from government publications

Lengthy documents and reports should be represented by copies of their title pages, tables of contents, and a one-page summary (or abstract) of the document either taken from the document itself or written by the group. Be sure to include a table of contents for this section.

FORM 10

INSTRUCTIONS FOR CONSTITUTIONAL OPINION FORM

Whenever we suggest that government adopt a public policy to deal with a problem, it is important that the policy we suggest

- serves one or more of the purposes of government set forth in our U.S. Constitution and
- does not ask government to do something prohibited by the U.S. Constitution.

The Constitutional Opinion Form includes some of the most important purposes our U.S. Constitution sets forth for our government. It also includes some of the most important limitations the Constitution places upon government. Use the form when you develop your proposed public policy. Be sure that your policy serves the purposes of government and does not violate the limits placed on government that are designed to protect individual rights.

This Constitutional Opinion Form should be included in Part 3 of the display and documentation sections of your portfolio. Use this form to prepare a summary statement for both parts of your portfolio. The statement should support your position that your proposed public policy serves the purposes of government and does not violate rights protected by the U.S. Constitution.

Purposes of government Explain which, if any, of the following purposes of government from the Declaration of Independence and the Preamble to the Constitution would be served by your proposed policy.

- Securing the unalienable rights of individuals, such as those to life, liberty, property, and the pursuit of happiness
- Establishing justice
- Providing for individual security and public order
- Protecting the people from harm from internal and external sources
- Providing for the general welfare (or the common good)

Limitations on government to protect individual rights The following are some of the basic rights of individuals and limitations placed on government by the U.S. Constitution and Bill of Rights that are designed to protect those rights. If your proposed policy might appear to interfere with one or more of these rights, justify your position by explaining why you think what you are proposing is reasonable and fair and would not violate the U.S. Constitution.

- **The right to freedom of religion** The government cannot make any laws that place unreasonable and unfair limits on a person's freedom to practice his or her religion.
- **The right to freedom of expression** The government cannot make any laws that place unreasonable and unfair limits on a person's right to express him- or herself in speech, writing, or by other means.
- **The right to due process of law (fair procedures)** The government cannot take a person's life, liberty, or property without giving that person a fair hearing in a court of law or before another authorized agency of government.
- **The right to privacy** Privacy is the right to be let alone. The government cannot invade the privacy of a person's home or interfere in other private matters without having a compelling reason for doing so.
- **The right to equality of opportunity** The government cannot unreasonably or unfairly discriminate against people on the basis of race, religion, age, ethnic group (national origin), or gender.

FORM 11

CONSTITUTIONAL OPINION FORM

1 **OUR PROPOSED POLICY SERVES THE FOLLOWING PURPOSES OF GOVERNMENT**

- ☐ Securing the rights of individuals
- ☐ Establishing justice
- ☐ Providing for security and public order
- ☐ Protecting the people from harm
- ☐ Providing for the general welfare

Explain ▶

2 **OUR PROPOSED POLICY RESPECTS THE FOLLOWING INDIVIDUAL RIGHTS**

- ☐ The right to freedom of religion
- ☐ The right to freedom of expression
- ☐ The right to due process of law
- ☐ The right to privacy
- ☐ The right to equality of opportunity

Explain ▶

FORM 11

CONSTITUTIONAL OPINION FORM (CONTINUED)

3 Government is not allowed to interfere with a person's freedom of belief. Our proposed public policy (does/does not) violate this limit on the power of government. Explain why.

____

____

____

____

4 Government is not allowed to place unreasonable and unfair limits on a person's right to express him- or herself in speech, writing, or by other means. Our proposed public policy (does/does not) violate this limit on the power of government. Explain why.

____

____

____

____

5 Government is not allowed to take a person's life, liberty, or property without giving that person a fair hearing in a court of law or before another authorized agency of government. Our proposed public policy (does/does not) violate this limit on the power of government. Explain why.

____

____

____

____

6 Government is not allowed to invade the privacy of a person's home without a very good reason for doing so. Our proposed public policy (does/does not) violate this limit on the power of government. Explain why.

____

____

____

____

7 Government is not allowed to make laws that unreasonably or unfairly discriminate against people on the basis of race, religion, age, ethnic group (national origin), or gender. Our proposed public policy (does/does not) violate this limit on the power of government. Explain why.

____

____

____

____

Summary Statement

Write a summary statement in which you support your belief that your proposed public policy does not violate the Constitution or interfere with these rights.

____

____

____

____

ANNIHALATE
SMOKING IN
PUBLIC
BUILDINGS
WHY
no exceptions
YOU DON'T HAVE TO BREATHE OTHER PEOPLE'S SMOKE
DON'T EVEN THINK OF SMOKING HERE
NO SMOKING WITHIN 15 FEET OF ANYWHERE
ALTERNATIVE POLICY
CLASS POLICY
ACTION PLAN
NO SMOKING
ARKANSAS

DISCOVERY NATURE TRAIL: A SAFE PLACE TO RIDE
PROBLEM
ALTERNATIVES
OUR POLICY
PLAN OF ACTION
MISSISSIPPI

HIGH SCHOOL FAILURES ON THE RISE
PROBLEM
ROAD TO NOWHERE
One Size Does Not Fit All
YIELD
ALTERNATIVE
CLASS POLICY
Schools have to change!
OUR PLAN
100%
ROAD TO THE NEW MILLENIUM
KEY
TO CHANGE
The Winner is You!
Connecting
ACTION PLAN
SAY NO TO HIGH SCHOOL FAILURES!
FINALIST
MICHIGAN

PORTFOLIO GROUP 4

DEVELOPING AN ACTION PLAN

This group is responsible for developing an action plan for getting your proposed public policy adopted and implemented by government. The plan should include all of the steps that would be necessary. Your group will explain the action plan in the display section and in the documentation section of your class, or small group, portfolio.

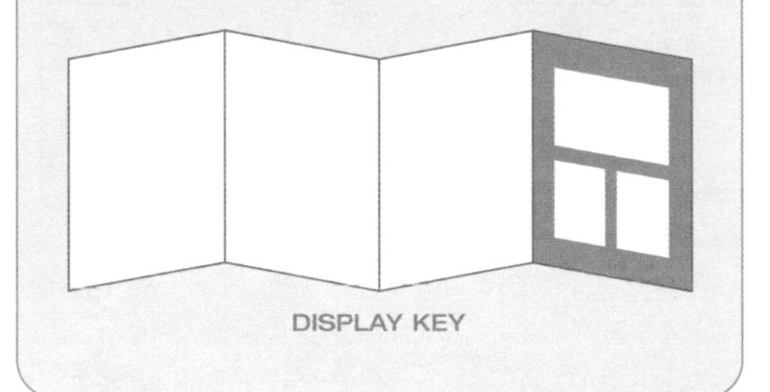

DISPLAY KEY

A DISPLAY SECTION 4

This part should include the following items:

1 **A written explanation of how your class could develop support for your proposed public policy among individuals and groups in your community**
On one double-spaced typed page/script, describe the main points of your policy and your action plan to get it adopted. Be sure to

- identify influential individuals and groups in your community who might be willing to support your proposed public policy, and briefly describe how you might gain their support
- identify groups in your community that might oppose your proposed public policy, and explain how you might convince them to support it

2 **A written explanation of your action plan for gaining support from your government for your proposed public policy**
On one double-spaced typed page, describe the main points of your plan. Be sure to

- identify influential government officials and agencies that might be willing to support your proposed public policy, and briefly describe how you will get them to support it
- identify people in government who might oppose your proposed public policy, and explain how you might convince them to support it

3 **Graphic presentations of your action plan**
These may include charts, graphs, photos, drawings, political cartoons, newspaper headlines, tables of statistics, and other illustrations. These illustrations may come from printed sources or they may be your original creations. Each illustration should have a caption or title and where appropriate, a source citation.

4 **Identification of your sources of information**
Include a bibliography identifying all sources used.

Regardless of the presentation format your class or small group chooses to present its work, you will need to create a documentation section in the form of a three-ring binder that includes the best or most important information your class, or group, gathered and used in developing your action plan.

For example, you may include as documentation

- selected statements by influential individuals and groups
- statements by influential government officials and agencies
- newspaper or magazine clippings
- written reports of interviews with people in the community
- written reports of radio and television coverage of the problem
- communications from public and private interest groups
- excerpts from government publications

Lengthy documents and reports should be represented by copies of their title pages, tables of contents, and a one-page summary (or abstract) of the document either taken from the document itself or written by the group.

PROBLEM
ALTERNATIVE POLICIES
CLASS POLICY
ACTION PLAN

STEP 5

Presenting Your Portfolio in a Simulated Public Hearing

PURPOSE

When your portfolio is completed, you should prepare to present your work before an audience in a simulated public hearing. The way this simulation is structured is similar to the way actual testimony from speakers and expert witnesses is presented in public meetings before committees or boards of legislative and executive branches of government.

Your teacher should arrange for your class to make a presentation before a panel of several members of your school and community. The panel members will evaluate your presentation based on the same criteria you used to develop your portfolio. This activity will give you valuable experience in presenting important ideas to others and convincing them of your position.

A What Are the Goals of the Simulated Public Hearing?

There are four basic goals of your class presentation:

- to explain the importance of the problem you have studied
- to explain and evaluate the advantages and disadvantages of alternative polices designed to deal with the problem you have selected
- to explain why your proposed public policy is the best way to deal with the problem and to "make the case" for the adoption and implementation of your proposed policy. In doing so, you should explain why your proposed policy does not violate your state and federal constitutions
- to explain how your proposed action plan is designed to get governmental officials to adopt and implement your policy

Each of these goals matches a task that one of the four portfolio groups had responsibility for when developing your class portfolio. During the presentation, each group will be responsible for fulfilling its goal using the following guidelines.

B Opening Oral Presentation

Each of the four portfolio groups will have an opportunity to present its work in sequence before a panel of members of their school or community. The first four minutes of each group's presentation will be a prepared opening statement during which the group members orally present the most significant information from their part of the portfolio.

The prepared statement should be based on the research presented in the portfolio display and documentation sections, but should not be a word for word reading from the portfolio. Each member of the group should have a role in this part of the presentation. Presenters may refer to notes or written prepared statements in this part of their presentation.

Presenters may refer to graphics or other materials in their portfolio to help explain or emphasize a point. Only information and materials included in the display or documentation sections of portfolios may be used during the oral presentation.

C Follow-up Questions

The next six minutes of each group's presentation will be a follow-up question period during which the panel will ask questions about the group's research as presented in the portfolio and in the opening statement. During this period the panelists might ask students to

- explain further or clarify points they have made
- give examples of specific points they have made
- defend some of their statements or positions
- explain how they arrived at positions they have taken or conclusions they have drawn

D Preparation

It is important that your class spend some time preparing before actually presenting in a simulated public hearing. To get ready you might

- have each portfolio group practice its oral presentation prior to giving it to an audience; try it out in front of students from your class, other classes, or a panel of teachers or parents
- attend in person, or watch on C-SPAN or your local or state government cable channels, several public meetings or legislative committee hearings to see how the are done
- ask parents or other community members experienced in making public presentations to coach your group; people involved in local government or in civic and community organizations can be very helpful

E Guidelines for the Presentation

As many members as possible of each group should participate in the opening presentation and follow-up question period. One or two students should not dominate the oral presentation. It should demonstrate the cooperative learning that went into the portfolio preparation.

Do not read to the panel members from your portfolio. Select the most important information and arguments and present them in a conversational style.

You may use notes or a written prepared statement during the opening presentation but not during the follow-up question period.

If you do not use the full four minutes allowed for the opening presentation, the unused time will be added to the follow-up question period. Each portfolio group will have a total of ten minutes before the panel.

F Evaluation Criteria

Your teacher may arrange for the panel members to provide numerical and written evaluation of your portfolio and your oral presentation. Your teacher will explain to the panelists the criteria to be used in these evaluations. The evaluation instruments that they will use will be the same as those used as a self-evaluation during the development of your portfolio (see the Portfolio Criteria Checklist on pages 58–59).

G Presenting Your Ideas to the Government Officials Who Make Policy Decisions

After you have presented your portfolio and your research to an audience in a simulated public hearing, you may wish to arrange to present your proposed public policy before the government officials who would decide on policy related to the problem you studied. Your teacher, or other adults you have worked with on your project, may be willing to help you to arrange a private hearing or to get on the agenda at a public hearing. This will give you an opportunity to exercise your rights as citizens and at the same time practice civic responsibility by actively participating in the governance of your community.

STEP 6

Reflecting on Your Experience

PURPOSE

At first glance, it might appear that Project Citizen is almost entirely about procedures or process and that there is very little content to be gained by taking part in the program. By the time you have reached this step in the program, you should be aware that much of the "content" of Project Citizen is implicit and much is gained from the experiences you have had in fulfilling the tasks of the program. This content may become more apparent if you reflect upon your experiences. By doing so you should realize, for example, that you have been exercising many of the rights and fulfilling many of the responsibilities of citizens in a democracy. You have also been expecting public officials to act in accordance with democratic principles, learning something about the importance of civil society, and learning some of the roles and responsibilities of governmental agencies at local or state or federal levels. This step calls upon you to reflect upon and record such learning in a report that you will include in Part 5 of your documentation binder.

A Critical Thinking Exercise Identifying Some of the Content of Project Citizen

Your class will work in four groups. Each group should discuss and record its responses to two of the following questions, e.g., Group 1— questions 1 and 2; Group 2— questions 3 and 4, etc. Each group should also answer question 9. After completing your group work, you should share and discuss your responses with the class. The recorded responses of the four groups should be added as Part 5 of your documentation binder.

1. What purposes of government was your proposed public policy designed to serve?
2. What rights and responsibilities of citizens of a democracy did you exercise when you were fulfilling the tasks of Project Citizen? For example, what rights and responsibilities were involved when you
    - identified public policy problems in your communities?
    - discussed these problems with each other and with members of your family and other adults?
    - decided which problem to study by reaching consensus or voting?
    - gathered information on the problem from various sources?
    - evaluated alternative solutions to the problem?
    - proposed a solution to the problem?
    - checked your solution according to constitutional principles?
    - developed an action plan to use in getting your government to consider your solution to the problem?
    - presented your portfolio to a panel of adults?
3. Which, if any, of the following purposes of government in a democracy would your proposed policy help to fulfill? Explain your answers.
    - Protecting the rights of individuals to life, liberty, and property
    - Promoting the common good
    - Promoting justice or fairness, including equal opportunities for all people
    - Providing safety and security

4 What have you learned about how your government is organized and the responsibilities of various agencies of government? For example, what agencies at local or state or national levels did you find that are responsible for

- making laws
- carrying out or administering laws
- enforcing laws
- managing disputes over the application of laws
- making sure citizens can see what their government is doing
- making sure public officials use fair procedures (due process of law) when they are gathering information and making decisions

5 What responsibilities of public officials in a democracy did you learn about when you were fulfilling the tasks of Project Citizen? For example, what responsibilities of public officials were involved when you asked them

- for information about the problem you had chosen?
- who in your government was responsible for dealing with such problems?
- what their responsibilities were?
- to listen to your opinions about the problem?
- to accept your proposed public policy solution to the problem?

6 When you gathered information on the problem you selected, you may have found out about groups and organizations in civil society that were also interested in your problem.

- What were the purposes and interests of each of the groups you identified?
- How did these groups try to monitor and influence government?
- What advantages do people gain from joining such groups?
- What role do such groups play in a democracy?

7 The following is a list of some of the fundamental values and principles of democracy. List any of the values and principles that were related to the public policy you suggested and the experiences you had in fulfilling the tasks of Project Citizen. Explain the relationship.

- **Values**
  - Individual rights
    - Life, including quality of life
    - Liberty or freedom
    - Justice
    - Equality
    - Diversity
    - Truth
  - Common good
- **Principles**
  - Popular sovereignty — the people as the ultimate source of authority of government
  - Constitutional government
  - Rule of law
  - Separation of powers
  - Checks and balances
  - Minority rights
  - Judicial review

8 The following is a list of attitudes and character traits of citizens that are important in a democracy. List any that were related to the experiences you had in fulfilling the tasks of Project Citizen. Then explain how they were involved and how they might be important to a democracy.

- Individual responsibility
- Self discipline/self-governance
- Civility
- Courage
- Respect for the rights of other individuals
- Respect for law
- Honesty
- Open-mindedness
- Critical-mindedness
- Negotiation and compromise
- Persistence
- Civic-mindedness
- Compassion
- Patriotism

9 What did you gain from your experiences in fulfilling the tasks of Project Citizen?

- What skills did you gain or improve?
- What did you learn about the advantages and disadvantages of working cooperatively?
- What do you think you did well?
- What improvements might be helpful if you were to participate in Project Citizen–type activities again?

CHAPTER 4

Why Is Citizen Participation Important to Democracy?

PURPOSE

The purpose of this final chapter is to help you understand why citizen participation is important to democracy. You will discuss the importance of participation, how people can participate, and the possible consequences of low citizen participation in a democracy.

A Group Activity—Examining the Roles and Responsibilities of Citizens in a Democracy

The following three quotations address some of the roles and responsibilities of citizens and their government in a democracy. Your class will work in three or more groups. Each group should read one of the quotations and respond to the questions that follow it. Groups should then prepare to present and discuss their answers with the entire class.

Group 1

> *If liberty and equality, as is thought by some, are chiefly to be found in a democracy, they will be attained when all persons alike share in the government to the utmost.*
>
> *Aristotle,* Politics *(c. 340 B.C.)*

1. What argument can you make to support the idea that "all persons alike" must "share in the government to the utmost" in a democracy for liberty and equality to flourish?
2. If "all persons alike" must "share in the government to the utmost" in a democracy for liberty and equality to flourish, what responsibilities of citizens does this imply?
3. What argument can you make to support the idea that liberty and equality are more likely to be found in a democracy than in another form of government?
4. Do you agree with Aristotle's statement? Why or why not?

Group 2

I know of no safe depository of the ultimate powers of the society but the people themselves; and if we think them not enlightened enough to exercise their control with a wholesome discretion, the remedy is not to take it from them, but to inform their discretion.

Thomas Jefferson (1820)

1. What argument can you make to support the idea that the ultimate powers of society should be placed in the hands of the people instead of an elite group of knowledgeable people?
2. If the ultimate powers of the society are placed in the hands of the people, what responsibilities does this imply for individuals and the people as a whole?
3. What might be the consequences for democracy if a large number of people are "not enlightened enough to exercise their control with a wholesome discretion"?
4. What responsibilities does this imply for citizens and their government?

Group 3

Never doubt that a small group of thoughtful, committed citizens can change the world; indeed, it is the only thing that ever does.

Margaret Mead (1901–1978)

1. What arguments can you give for and against this statement?
2. What examples can you give of small groups of citizens making significant changes in their communities, states, nations, or the world? How were they able to achieve their goals?
3. What steps would you take if you wanted to make a significant change in your community? Do you think it might be possible for you to do so? Why or why not?

B What Are the Roles of Citizens in a Democracy?

As you learned in previous steps, it is important for citizens to work together to develop and support public policy solutions to problems that face their communities. You have learned how to monitor and influence public policy decisions. You may even have been successful in getting your proposed policy considered or adopted by public officials. Even if you tried and your policy was not considered or adopted, however, you have acquired valuable knowledge and important skills that will enable you to become a more competent and responsible participant in our constitutional democracy.

C Critical Thinking Exercise

The following are the same questions that you answered in Chapter 1. Without looking back to see what you wrote then, answer the questions again now that you have completed the Project Citizen program. Compare your answers before and after the program and discuss them with your class.

Conclusion

It is important for all citizens to increase their knowledge and develop the skills that will enhance their ability to monitor and influence the development and implementation of public policy. Public policies need to be monitored by citizens and sometimes need to be revised. New problems, interests, or goals may require new public policies. Having a voice in the development and implementation of public policies is a right and responsibility of all citizens in a self-governing society.

The sponsors of Project Citizen hope that the experiences and learning it has fostered will encourage you to take an active role in the political life of your community, state, and nation. If the United States is to fulfill its historic mission of being a nation "by the people, for the people, and dedicated to liberty and justice for all," it is essential for you to take a part in your system of self-government.

WHAT DO YOU THINK?

1. To what extent, if any, do citizens have a responsibility to take part in the civic life of their community?

   a no responsibility

   b some responsibility

   c a large responsibility

   d a very large responsibility

   Explain your answer.

2. To what extent, if any, do citizens have a responsibility to participate in the public policymaking processes at local, state, and national levels?

   a no responsibility

   b some responsibility

   c a large responsibility

   d a very large responsibility

   Explain your answer.

3. What can citizens do to monitor the development and implementation of public policy in their community?

4. What can citizens do to influence the development and implementation of public policy in their community?

5. How can citizens gain access to governmental agencies in their communities, their states, and the nation?

6. In what ways can the voluntary organizations of civil society participate in the formulation and in some instances in the implementation of public policy?

7. What might be some consequences of an individual deciding not to participate in civic life? What might be the consequences if large numbers of individuals do not participate in civic life?

Cover photo Kathleen Card, Natural Light Photography, © 2006 Center for Civic Education; page 1, Meeting of the Council of the District of Columbia, photo courtesy of John Windmueller, Ph.D., Assistant Professor, Center for Negotiations & Conflict Management, University of Baltimore; 8, U.S. Census Bureau; 11, Ed Edahl/FEMA; 18, Andrea Booher/FEMA; 19, © 2005 Center for Civic Education; 22, © 2003 Getty Images, Inc., photo by Pando Hall; 24, Greg Henshall/FEMA; 25, Ed Edahl/FEMA; 58, © 2004 Center for Civic Education; 61, © 2006 Center for Civic Education; 69a, © 2005 Center for Civic Education; 69b, © 2005 Center for Civic Education; 73, © 2006 Center for Civic Education; 81, AP Photo/Jay LaPrete; 82, Aristotle, photo courtesy of Martin Haase; 83a, *Thomas Jefferson* by Rembrandt Peale, Prints and Photographs Division, Library of Congress, LC-USZC4-2474; 83b, Dr. Margaret Mead, World-Telegram photo by Edward Lynch, Prints and Photographs Division, Library of Congress, LC-USZ62-120226.